PRAYER *and*
STUDY GUIDE

The Power of a
PRAYING®
WOMAN

STORMIE
OMARTIAN

HARVEST HOUSE PUBLISHERS

EUGENE, OREGON

Cover by Koechel Peterson & Associates, Minneapolis, Minnesota

THE POWER OF A PRAYING® WOMAN PRAYER AND STUDY GUIDE
Copyright © 2002 by Stormie Omartian
Published by Harvest House Publishers
Eugene, Oregon 97402
www.harvesthousepublishers.com

Library of Congress Cataloging-in-Publication Data
    ISBN-13: 978-0-7369-1987-6
    ISBN-10: 0-7369-1987-2

Printed in the United States of America

08 09 10 11 12 13 / BP-KB / 10 9 8 7 6 5 4 3

THIS BOOK BELONGS TO

_____

Please do not read beyond this page without permission of
the person named above.

————————

$\mathcal{A}$ supplemental workbook to
THE POWER OF A PRAYING WOMAN
by Stormie Omartian,
for in-depth group or individual study.

———— ✧ ✧ ————

Contents

What You Should Know Before You Start

his PRAYER AND STUDY GUIDE is designed to be a companion to THE POWER OF A PRAYING WOMAN book. As you answer the questions in each of the following chapters, you will be able to better understand what the truth of your situation is and how you can pray specifically about your life. Answering the questions will also help you to remember what God's promises are to you as you incorporate Scripture into your prayers.

What You Will Need

This 30-week plan for personal or group study can also be used as a 30-*day* plan if you have the time and desire to move forward at a more rapid pace. You will need to have the book THE POWER OF A PRAYING WOMAN and a Bible in which you feel free to write.

In All Honesty

While most of your answers will help you gain an understanding of the Scriptures pertaining to a specific area of prayer focus, many of them will reflect your own personal feelings, experiences, and needs. Be completely honest with yourself. There are no right or wrong answers, only *honest* answers. They will help you to determine exactly what your prayer needs are and enable you to think more clearly about how to pray about them. Write something for each question, even if it is only a sentence or two.

How to Proceed as a Group

If you are doing this book as a group, before each meeting read the designated chapter in THE POWER OF A PRAYING WOMAN and fill out the corresponding chapter in this PRAYER AND STUDY GUIDE. When the group comes together, the leader may go over some or all of the questions and ask what insights were gleaned and what God spoke to the heart of each woman as she read and wrote. Some women may feel led to share what their particular prayer needs are regarding this area of prayer focus. It's always encouraging to hear other women tell of their struggles and how they are overcoming them. It may even be that many of the members of the group will have similar prayer needs and so can pray for one another about them. However, no one should share more than they feel comfortable doing.

I recommend praying the suggested prayer together at the end of the chapter in the book and then embellishing it with individual requests. If the group is large, you may want to break into smaller groups of three to five women for the individual prayer requests. I encourage everyone to participate in the prayer time, even if it is praying only a few sentences. If it is difficult for you to pray aloud in front of others, you'll find that the more you do it, the easier it will become. Remember, God is not looking for eloquence, the perfect spiritual words, or volume (and neither is anyone else). He is looking for fervency and honesty of heart.

Praying a Scripture

It is very important that you understand there is great power in writing out a Scripture as a prayer or including Scripture in your prayers as you pray aloud. When you are asked in this book to write out a particular Scripture as a prayer, it is so that you will be able to appropriate and apply that Scripture to your own life. Doing this not only increases your knowledge and memory of what God's Word says and how it applies to you, but it also increases your faith. If you have never done that before, this is the way to do it. For example, Matthew 6:31-33 could be written out as a prayer like this:

"Lord, help me not to worry about what I will eat or drink or what I will wear. I realize that You know I need these things. Help me to, instead, seek first Your kingdom and Your righteousness, trusting that all these things will be given to me."

May this workbook help you to pray effectively and in depth about your life and the people you care about most. As you proceed, be prepared to see great things happen in both. Shall we get started?

$\mathscr{W}$EEK $\mathscr{O}$NE

Read "The Power" and Chapter 1:
"Lord, Draw Me into a Closer Walk with You"
from THE POWER OF A PRAYING WOMAN

Before you begin, ask God to help you be completely honest with yourself and with Him in answering these questions. Remember, He already knows the truth, and no one else should be reading this but you.

1. Do you feel you are growing mentally?_____.
   Emotionally?_____. Spiritually?_____.
   Explain each of your answers.

2. In what ways would you like to see yourself grow and develop in the future?

3. What are the greatest longings of your heart? What would satisfy those longings and desires? Do you believe it is God's will for you to have those desires met?

4. Do you find it harder to pray for yourself than you do for others? Explain why or why not.

5. We will never be happy until we make_____the source of our_____ and the_____ to our _____. He is the_____ _____ who should have_____over our_____.
(See page 14, first paragraph, in THE POWER OF A PRAYING WOMAN.)

6. Read 2 Corinthians 12:9 in your Bible and underline it. In light of this verse, why is it okay to feel weak?

7. What do you believe are some of your areas of weakness?
   (For example, it could be things such as public speaking,
   confronting issues, meeting new people, being organized,
   sharing your faith, getting along with others, handling finances, walking in faith, or resisting temptation.) Write
   out a prayer asking God to help you be strong in the areas
   where you are weak, if that is His will, or that His
   strength would be made perfect in your weakness.

8. Do you feel at this moment in your life that you are a sur-
   vivor, an overcomer, or somewhere in between? Explain.
   Write out a prayer asking God to help you transcend any
   particular circumstances or limitations in your life.

9. Read John 10:10 in your Bible and underline it. Do you
   believe you are living the abundant life Jesus is talking
   about here? (Spiritually? Relationally? Financially? Emotionally? Physically?) Explain your answer. In what ways
   would you like to see yourself move into the abundance
   God has for you?

10. Do you ever feel powerless in the face of your circumstances?

    Always_____ Often_____ Sometimes_____ Never_____

    Do you recognize your need for a power greater than yourself in your life?

    Always_____ Often_____ Sometimes_____ Never_____

    Do you believe that without God's power, you can't transcend your circumstances or see your life transformed?

    Always_____ Often_____ Sometimes_____ Never_____

    Do you sense that you have the Spirit of God living in you?

    Always_____ Often_____ Sometimes_____ Never_____

    Do you feel the power of God moving in your life?

    Always_____ Often_____ Sometimes_____ Never_____

    Do you long for more of the power of God to be manifested in your life?

    Always_____ Often_____ Sometimes_____ Never_____

    How often do you ask the Holy Spirit to move powerfully through you?

    Always_____ Often_____ Sometimes_____ Never_____

In light of your answers on the previous page, how could you pray about your relationship with the Holy Spirit? Write out that prayer below.

11. Read Ephesians 3:20-21 in your Bible and underline these verses. What is the promise to you in this portion of Scripture? What does this promise mean to you in terms of your level of faith and hope?

12. What are the prerequisite conditions for moving in the power of God? Have you met those conditions? When did you receive the Lord and make Him ruler of your life? (See page 17, second paragraph, in THE POWER OF A PRAYING WOMAN.)

13. Read the "Five Good Ways to Tell if Your Walk with God Is Shallow" on page 28 of THE POWER OF A PRAYING WOMAN. Write out the five signs that your relationship with God is growing deep.

1. _____

   _____.

2. _____

   _____.

3. _____

   _____.

4. _____

   _____.

5. _____

   _____.

In which of these ways would you most like to see your walk with the Lord grow deeper?

14. Do you have a hunger in your soul to know the Lord better and walk closer to Him? Write out a prayer below explaining your feelings about this to God.

15. Read James 4:8 in your Bible and underline it. In light of this Scripture, what do you need to do?

_____

_____

Write out a prayer to God asking Him to help you do those things.

16. Look up the Scriptures below regarding the ten names and attributes of the Lord mentioned, and write them out in the space provided.

    1. My Healer (Psalm 103:3)

    2. My Strength (Isaiah 12:2)

    3. My Peace (2 Thessalonians 3:16)

    4. My Counselor (Psalm 16:7)

    5. My Redeemer (Isaiah 59:20)

    6. My Shelter (Joel 3:16)

    7. My Provider (Genesis 22:14)

    8. My Deliverer (Psalm 70:5)

9. My Friend (John 15:15)

10. My Restorer (Psalm 23:3)

17. From the list of names to call your God on page 32 in THE
POWER OF A PRAYING WOMAN, what is the name you
most need to trust God to be to you during this time in
your life? _____. Write out a prayer
telling God why you need to know Him in this way, and
thank Him for promising to be that to you. In your prayer
include Psalm 20:7.

18. Do you spend as much time as you would like alone with
God?_____. Do you find securing that time alone
with God difficult or easy?_____. Write out a
prayer below asking God to help you find more time to be
with Him. Describe any difficulty you have.

19. Read Psalm 18:1-3 in your Bible and underline these verses. Write them out as a prayer from you to God. (For example: "I love You, Lord. You are my strength, my rock, my fortress...")

20. Pray the prayer out loud on pages 33-34 in THE POWER OF A PRAYING WOMAN. Write out two or three sentences from this prayer that are the most meaningful to you at this time in your life.

WEEK TWO

Read Chapter 2: "Lord, Cleanse Me and
Make My Heart Right Before You"
from THE POWER OF A PRAYING WOMAN

1. Read 1 John 1:9 in your Bible and underline it. What is
   the main reason we need to confess our sins to God?

2. Read Acts 3:19 in your Bible and underline it. What is
   the main reason we need to repent of our sins?

3. Read page 40, the first paragraph under "Full Repentance," in THE POWER OF A PRAYING WOMAN and describe what true repentance is.

4. Read Romans 6:23 in your Bible and underline it. What is the result of sin? _____.

   What is the gift of God? _____.

5. Read Proverbs 28:13 in your Bible and underline it. What happens to someone who covers up his sin? _____ _____. What happens to someone who confesses and forsakes his sin? _____.

6. Read 1 John 1:8 in your Bible and underline it. In light of this verse, can we say we are without sin? _____. If we say we are without sin, then what is true of us?_____ _____. Write a prayer asking God to

reveal any sin in your life, whether in thought, word, or action. Confess any sin you are aware of and ask God to show you anything you are not seeing. Ask God to keep you undeceived and cleanse you from all unrighteousness. Include Psalm 139:23-24 in your prayer.

7. The Bible says, "My conscience is clear, but that does not make me innocent" (1 Corinthians 4:4 NIV). Even though we don't feel bad about something we have done that is against God's ways, we will still pay the consequences for it. Write out a prayer asking God to show you if you have any sin in your life that you have somehow rationalized, explained away, or not understood to be sin. Read Psalm 19:12 and Psalm 51:10 in your Bible and underline them. Include them in your prayer. Confess any sin God reveals to you and ask Him to keep you free from *all* sin.

8. Read 1 John 3:21-22 in your Bible and underline these verses. Do you feel your heart is clean before the Lord? _____. Do you have any guilt, remorse, or regret about something you have done, said, or thought? _____. Explain. Write out a prayer asking God to make your heart completely right and clean before Him. Include Psalm 32:5 in your own words as part of the prayer.

9. Read Psalm 19:14 in your Bible and underline it. Write this Scripture out as a prayer.

10. Pray the prayer out loud on pages 41-42 in THE POWER OF A PRAYING WOMAN. Write out two or three sentences from this prayer that are the most meaningful to you at this time in your life.

$\mathcal{W}$EEK $\mathcal{T}$HREE

Read Chapter 3: "Lord, Help Me to Be a Forgiving Person"
from THE POWER OF A PRAYING WOMAN

1. Read Mark 11:25-26 in your Bible and underline these verses. What is the most important reason to forgive others?

2. Read 1 John 2:9-11 in your Bible and underline these verses. What is one way we can be walking in darkness in our lives? _____.

How can we walk in the light? _____

_____.

3. Read 1 John 2:11 again in your Bible. What happens to us when we hate someone and don't forgive them so we can release that hate? _____
_____.
Do you feel you are walking in the darkness or the light with regards to this issue in your life? Explain your answer.

4. Can you think of a time when someone said something bad, unkind, unflattering, dishonoring, or hurtful to you or about you? If so, describe your feelings about it now and whether you feel you have completely forgiven that person. If you are not sure you have completely forgiven that person, write out a prayer confessing your unforgiveness and asking God to help you forgive him or her completely.

5. Read Mark 11:25 again in your Bible. Has anyone ever done something offensive, disrespectful, or hurtful to you that you have not completely forgiven? Explain and write out a prayer asking God to help you forgive him or her completely. If you can't think of any particular person or incident, write out a prayer asking God to show you if there is any unforgiveness in you.

6. Read Exodus 20:12 in your Bible and underline it. Is there anything you need to forgive your father or mother for so that you can fully honor him or her and thereby extend the length and the quality of your own life? Explain. Write out a prayer confessing unforgiveness toward either parent and ask God to help you forgive him or her completely.

7. Do you have any family relationships that are strained or severed because of unforgiveness? If so, write out a prayer asking God to break down that wall. If not, write out a prayer asking God to preserve all of your family relationships and keep them from being strained by unforgiveness.

8. Have you ever said or done something that you still regret? Have you been able to forgive yourself for it? If so, explain. If not, write out a prayer asking God to forgive you and help you forgive yourself.

9. Read Matthew 5:44 in your Bible and underline it. Write it out below as a prayer. (For example, "Lord, I pray that You would help me to love my enemies, bless those who curse me...")

10. Pray the prayer out loud on pages 50-52 in THE POWER OF A PRAYING WOMAN. Write out two or three sentences that are the most meaningful to you at this time in your life.

$\mathcal{W}$EEK $\mathcal{F}$OUR

Read Chapter 4: "Lord, Teach Me to Walk in Obedience to Your Ways" from THE POWER OF A PRAYING WOMAN

1. Read Deuteronomy 11:8-9 and 26-27 in your Bible and underline them. According to these verses, what is the result of obeying God?

2. Read 1 Samuel 15:22 in your Bible and underline it. According to this Scripture, what is better than sacrifice? _____. Is there any area of your life where you know you are walking in disobedience to God's laws? If so, write out a prayer confessing it and asking God to help you not do that anymore. If you are *not* aware of any disobedience on your part, write out a prayer asking God to show you any way you are not living in obedience to His laws.

3. Read James 4:17 in your Bible and underline it. While you may not be walking in disobedience to God's laws, He may be speaking to you specifically about something He wants *you* to do. Is there any step of obedience you know God is requiring of you that you have not taken? _____. If you answered yes, write out a prayer asking God to help you obey Him in that area and take the steps you need to take. If you answered no, write out a prayer asking God to show you if there is anything He wants you to do or not do that you are not understanding. Write down what He shows you and ask Him to enable you to do it.

4. Is there any particular step of obedience you dislike doing, or are there any of God's laws that you have a particularly difficult time obeying? _____. Explain your answer.

5. Of the "Ten Good Reasons to Obey God" on pages 57-58 in THE POWER OF A PRAYING WOMAN, which three are the most important to you in terms of inspiring you to obey God's laws, even when you are tempted not to? Explain your answer.

6. Read 1 John 3:22 again in your Bible. Write this verse out below. Why is it important to obey God?

7. Read 1 John 2:4 in your Bible and underline it. What is the result of *not* keeping God's commandments?

8. Read John 14:21 in your Bible and underline it. What is the result of *keeping* God's commandments?

9. God's rules are for_____ _____, not to make us
   _____. When we live by them,_____
   _____. When we don't,_____ _____
   _____. When we obey, we have_____.
   When we don't, we have_____. And there is a
   definite connection between_____and
   the _____ of _____. (See page 59,
   the first paragraph, in THE POWER OF A PRAYING WOMAN.)

10. Pray the prayer out loud on page 60 in THE POWER OF A
    PRAYING WOMAN. Write out two or three sentences from
    this prayer that are the most meaningful to you at this
    time in your life.

WEEK FIVE

Read Chapter 5: "Lord, Strengthen Me to Stand Against the Enemy" from THE POWER OF A PRAYING WOMAN

1. Read Deuteronomy 31:6 in your Bible and underline it. Write this verse out as a prayer to the Lord. (For example, "Lord, help me to be strong...For You, O Lord, my God, are the One...")

2. Read Ephesians 6:10-11 and James 4:7 in your Bible and underline them. Write these two sections of Scripture out as a prayer. (For example, "Lord, help me to be strong in You...")

3. Read Ephesians 6:13-18 in your Bible and underline
   these verses. This is an extremely important Scripture for
   you to understand and be able to appropriate for your life
   as you stand strong against the enemy of your soul. Write
   these verses out as a prayer to God. (For example, "Lord,
   help me to take up the whole armor of God so that I will
   always be able to withstand the enemy. Help me to do all
   I need to do to stand strong. Help me to gird my waist
   with truth...")

4. We are all involved in a_____ _____
   with an_____ who will never_____ _____.
   Even though it is_____ who do_____
   _____ to us, we have to keep in mind that it
   is our ultimate enemy,_____ _____, who
   is behind it. "For we do not _____against
   _____ _____ _____, but against
   _____, against_____,
   against the_____of the_____
   _____ _____ _____, against _____
   _____ ___ _____ in
   the_____ places." (See page 64, first paragraph,
   in THE POWER OF A PRAYING WOMAN.

5. List the five powerful weapons God has given us to use
   against the enemy. (See pages 65-66 in THE POWER OF A
   PRAYING WOMAN.)

   1. _____.

   2. _____.

   3. _____.

   4. _____.

   5. _____.

6. Of those five weapons against the enemy, which one of
   them do you feel you most need to learn to use more effectively? Write out a prayer asking God to help you do that.

7. Write out a prayer asking God to help you use each one of these five weapons against the devil with utmost efficiency. Name each weapon.

8. Is there any place in your life where you are being worn down with worry, confusion, guilt, strife, sickness, fear, discouragement, depression, or defeat? Do you feel overwhelmed or burdened? Are you oppressed in your mind, emotions, health, work, or relationships? Do you ever feel like giving up? Explain and describe any area of your life where you feel the enemy might be attacking you. Then write out a prayer thanking God that He has given you the power, strength, and tools to stand against the enemy's attack. Thank Him that when you are in the heat of the battle, He will fight it for you and you will enjoy the victory together.

9. Write out a prayer asking God to keep you from being deceived by the enemy. Pray that the enemy will never be able to convince you that he is winning the battle. Ask God to show you any place where the enemy is robbing you of the abundance Jesus has promised you. (Remember that abundance in the Lord doesn't just imply money. It means health, fulfillment, peace, love, joy, contentment, relationships, fruitfulness, and success.)

10. Pray the prayer out loud on page 68 in THE POWER OF A PRAYING WOMAN. Write out two or three sentences from this prayer that are the most meaningful to you at this time in your life.

$\mathscr{W}$EEK $\mathscr{S}$IX

Read Chapter 6: "Lord, Show Me How to Take Control of My Mind" from THE POWER OF A PRAYING WOMAN

1. Read Romans 12:2 and Ephesians 4:22-24 in your Bible and underline these sections of Scripture. Write them out as a prayer to God. (For example, "Lord, help me to not be conformed to this world, but to be transformed by the...")

2. As you examine the verses mentioned on the previous page, what is the common thread in them?

3. Read John 8:44 in your Bible and underline it. Write out the description of the devil that Jesus gives.

4. What are some things that tempt you in your thought life? For example, are you tempted to think critically of a certain person? Are you tempted to think repeatedly about something offensive that happened to you in the past that makes you angry, unforgiving, or bitter? Are you tempted to think thoughts that are sexual in nature about someone to whom you are not married? Are these thoughts you *choose* to have or *want* to have? Explain. Everyone gets tempted in their thought life, so don't be hesitant to admit the truth to yourself.

5. Can you identify a reoccurring habit of thought in yourself that you don't like? Do you have negative thoughts about yourself? Describe them. Then write out a prayer asking God to break that pattern in you and set you free from the grip of it. If you can't think of anything like that, write out a prayer asking God to keep your mind free from any habits or thoughts that are not glorifying to Him.

6. Read 2 Corinthians 10:3-5 in your Bible and underline these verses. In light of this portion of Scripture write out a prayer asking God to help you take control of your mind and bring every thought into captivity.

7. Do you ever have thoughts that come into your mind that produce a certain feeling in your body such as weakness, queasiness, nausea, tightness in the throat, or a rash? Have you ever had bizarre or repulsive thoughts come to your mind that you don't want to have? Describe them in detail and then write out a prayer asking God to take away each one of these thoughts and replace them with thoughts of Him and His goodness.

8. Read John 8:47 in your Bible. Whose voice do you hear when you walk closely with the Lord?_____ Why do some people not hear God's voice?_____
_____
Do you ever sense God speaking to your heart? Explain.

9. Answer the following questions:

- Do you believe that you have a choice about what you will or will not accept as truth in your mind?

  Yes_____ No _____

- Do you understand that if *you* won't take control of your mind, you give the devil an opportunity to do so?

  Yes_____ No _____

- Do you see that having negative thoughts about yourself is not indicative of God giving you revelation for your life?

  Yes_____ No _____

- Do you understand that some of the negative thoughts about yourself may actually be the enemy trying to take control of your mind?

  Yes_____ No _____

- Do you ever remember believing a lie about yourself or your circumstances that you later realized was not true at all?

  Yes_____ No _____

- Do you know that it is possible to suffer greatly because of a lie you have accepted as truth?

  Yes_____ No _____

- Do you recognize that one of the enemy's tactics is to try and steal God's Word from you in some way and get you to doubt or question it?

  Yes_____ No _____

If you answered no to any of the questions on the previous page, write out a prayer asking God to help you recognize the lies of the enemy and learn to understand and believe only God's truth. Include in your prayer anything that your answers to the above questions revealed to you. If you answered yes to all of these questions, write out a prayer thanking God for giving you understanding and discernment. Ask Him to help you always keep your mind filled with His truth so you can identify the lies of the enemy.

10. Pray the prayer out loud on page 76 in THE POWER OF A PRAYING WOMAN. Write out two or three sentences from this prayer that are the most meaningful to you at this time in your life.

$\mathcal{W}$EEK $\mathcal{S}$EVEN

Read Chapter 7: "Lord, Rule Me in Every Area of My Life"
from THE POWER OF A PRAYING WOMAN

1. Read 1 Peter 5:6-7 in your Bible and underline these
   verses. Do you feel you have totally surrendered your life
   to God and humbled yourself under His mighty
   hand?_____. If you answered no to that question, write
   out a prayer below surrendering your life to Him now. If
   you answered yes, write out a prayer telling God of your
   renewed commitment to living your life completely surrendered to Him.

2. Are you willing to say yes to God no matter what He asks
   you to do?_____. If you answered yes, explain why. If
   you answered no, explain why and write out a prayer
   asking God to help you trust Him enough to do that.

3. Answer the following questions about your life:

Do you feel you are not having breakthrough in a certain area of your life? _____. Does it ever feel as though you can't get beyond the survival mode? _____. Do you experience one problem after another without end? _____. Do you sometimes feel you can't move forward in your life? _____.

If you answered yes to any of these questions, write out a prayer asking God if there is any area of your life you have not surrendered to Him. If you answered no to all of these questions, write out a prayer of thanksgiving to God and ask Him to help you stay totally surrendered to Him.

4. God is not only Lord over the_____, He is Lord over our_____ _____ as well. Whether we acknowledge that or not will determine the_____ and _____ of our life. If we don't personally declare Jesus to be _____ over our_____, it shows we are not _____ by the_____. "No one can say that _____ is_____ except by the _____ _____." (See page 80, second paragraph, in THE POWER OF A PRAYING WOMAN.)

5. Read Zechariah 7:12-13 in your Bible and underline these verses. In the New International Version of this section of Scripture, God says "When I called they did not listen, so when *they* called, *I* would not listen" (italics mine). According to these verses, what should we do if we want God to hear our prayers? What does this mean when God asks us to do a particular thing? Explain.

6. Read Jeremiah 17:9 in your Bible and underline it. What does this Scripture say about the human heart?

_____

_____. We all have blind spots and can be deceived and not see the truth about our thoughts, actions, and lives. Write out a prayer below asking God to show you if you are being deceived in any way. Ask Him to open your eyes and keep you undeceived. Ask Him to bring people into your life who will help you see the truth clearly.

7. Read Luke 16:10 in your Bible and underline it. What can happen to us when we think the little things don't matter and we allow ourselves to permit or rationalize "small" sins in our lives instead of requiring ourselves to be accountable and staying truly surrendered to God?

   _____. What happens when we are faithful in even the smallest ways? _____

   _____.

   Write out a prayer asking God to show you any way in which you are not being faithful, trustworthy, or surrendered to Him in your thoughts or actions.

8. Read Colossians 1:28 in your Bible and underline it. Why do we need to be taught by other strong believers in our lives?_____

   _____.

   Do you have any strong believers in your life who can help you discern wrong thoughts, actions, or decisions and help you stay on the right path? If so, explain. If not, write out a prayer asking God to help you get plugged in with people who can speak the truth in love to you.

9. Read Luke 9:23-24 in your Bible and underline these verses. Write out a prayer asking God to show you any place where you are trying to hang on to your life and not surrender it to Him. Write down anything He reveals to you. Ask Him to help you lose yourself in Him so that He can rule you and be Lord over every area of your life.

10. Pray the prayer out loud on page 82 in THE POWER OF A
    PRAYING WOMAN. Write out two or three sentences from
    this prayer that are the most meaningful to you at this
    time in your life.

$\mathcal{W}$EEK $\mathcal{E}$IGHT

Read Chapter 8: "Lord, Take Me Deeper in Your Word"
from THE POWER OF A PRAYING WOMAN

1. Read Psalm 1:1-3 in your Bible and underline these
   verses. Write out this section of Scripture in your own
   words and explain what it means to you.

2. Read James 1:22-25 in your Bible and underline these verses. Why is it important to *do* the Word and not just read it or hear it?

3. Do you believe God will speak to you personally through His Word? _____. Do you believe God will keep His promises to you that are found in His Word? _____. If so, write out a prayer of thanks to Him for doing that. If you have doubts about that, write out a prayer asking God to give you faith to believe for those things.

4. Look up the following Scriptures in your Bible and underline them. Write them out below, and as you do, ask God to let them become etched in your mind and soul.

• Psalm 119:11

• Matthew 4:4

• Psalm 19:7

• Joshua 1:8

• Romans 10:17

• Hebrews 4:12

5. Of the "Ten Good Reasons to Read God's Word" found on page 89 in THE POWER OF A PRAYING WOMAN, what are the three most important reasons to you right now? Explain why.

6. After writing the Scriptures on the previous page, what has God spoken to your heart about the power of His Word? Explain.

7. Read Isaiah 40:8 in your Bible and underline it. What does this verse mean to your faith in God's Word and His promises to you? Explain.

8. Read Romans 15:4 in your Bible and underline it. Write out a prayer asking God to give you patience, comfort, and hope every time you read His Word.

9. What is your greatest desire or frustration with regard to reading the Bible? (For example, "I wish I could understand it better." "I wish I could remember it better." "I would like to have more time to read it.") Explain in detail and then write out a prayer asking God for the very thing you need most regarding His Word.

10. Pray the prayer out loud on pages 90-91 in THE POWER OF A PRAYING WOMAN. Write out two or three sentences from this prayer that are the most meaningful to you at this time in your life.

WEEK NINE

Read Chapter 9: "Lord, Instruct Me As I Put My Life in Right Order" from THE POWER OF A PRAYING WOMAN

1. Read Matthew 22:37-39 in your Bible and underline these verses. What are the two top priorities supposed to be in your life? In light of these Scriptures, do you feel that you have your priorities in order? Explain.

2. Read Hebrews 13:17 in your Bible and underline it. Have you ever submitted to someone who violated your trust in any way? How did you react to it? How do you feel about the issue of submission? Explain.

3. Read Matthew 6:33 in your Bible and underline it. What is the first step you need to take before you can receive from God? _____. Do you do that on a daily basis? _____.
Write out a prayer asking God to help you remember to seek Him first for everything in your life so you can put your life in right order.

4. What are the names of the persons you are submitted to? (For example, husband, pastor, boss, manager, or group leader.) Is there anyone on that list you find especially difficult to submit to? Explain. Write out a prayer asking God to help you have a submissive heart toward that person.

5. Do you believe you are in the church where you belong at this time in your life? _____. Explain your answer. Write out a prayer asking God to show you clearly if you are in the church where He wants you to be. Ask Him to help you have total peace regarding this so you can receive all God has for you there.

6. Do you have a pastor, a strong Christian leader, or a godly mentoring person speaking truth into your life? _____. If you said yes, explain who that is and how they encourage you in the things of God. If you said no, write out a prayer asking God to bring someone into your life who will enrich your walk with the Lord and to whom you can be accountable.

7. Write a list below of all the things you want to do in the next three months to make your life more organized and in order. (For example, clean out a closet, hold a garage sale, reorganize your desk, reorganize your life, make that trip to visit your aunt before she gets too old to remember who you are, write a thank-you note, make necessary phone calls, attend a class, get into a Bible study, find a prayer partner, set aside time to pray more, and so on.) Circle any of the things you have listed which you find especially difficult or are unmotivated to do.

8. Pick three of the most important things from the list on the previous page and write out a prayer asking God to help you get those things done. Be specific. Pray that prayer every day until you actually accomplish them. Quite often just the act of writing these things down and praying about them will be all you need to get yourself moving and get them done.

9. List the top ten priorities in your life. (For example, spending time with God, praying, reading the Word, ministering to your husband, taking care of your children, doing things to better your health, doing well at your work, spending time helping friends, ministering to people in need, getting rest, and so on.)

Now, write out a prayer asking God to show you what your priorities are *supposed* to be and what order they *should* be in. Ask Him to reveal anything that is out of order or that should or should not be a priority in your life.

Pray the prayer you wrote above every day this week and see if God reveals anything new to you or brings clarity you didn't have before. Write below whatever God shows you that enhances or alters the list you wrote at the beginning of this section.

10. Pray the prayer out loud on pages 101-102 in THE POWER OF A PRAYING WOMAN. Write out two or three sentences from this prayer that are the most meaningful to you at this time in your life.

$\mathcal{W}$EEK $\mathcal{T}$EN

Read Chapter 10:
"Lord, Prepare Me to Be a True Worshiper"
from THE POWER OF A PRAYING WOMAN

1. Read Psalm 103 in your Bible and underline the things in that psalm for which you are most thankful. Write out a prayer below praising God for those promises and list the ten that are most important to you.

2. Read Romans 1:21 in your Bible and underline it. What can happen to you if you don't worship and glorify God?

3. What are five ways to praise the Lord? (See page 106 in THE POWER OF A PRAYING WOMAN.)

   1. _____.

   2. _____.

   3. _____.

   4. _____.

   5. _____.

4. Of those five ways to praise the Lord, which are you most comfortable doing? _____
   _____. Which are you least comfortable doing? _____.
   Write out a prayer asking God to help you become the true worshiper He wants you to be.

5. Read Psalm 9:9-10 in your Bible and underline these verses. Write a prayer of praise and thanksgiving to God listing all the reasons to praise Him contained in these verses. (For example, "Lord, I praise You and thank You that You are a refuge for the oppressed...")

6. Read Psalm 95:6-7 in your Bible and underline these verses. According to this section of Scripture what is another way to worship God and what are the reasons for doing so?

7. Read 2 Corinthians 3:17-18 in your Bible and underline these verses. What happens when we behold the Lord, which is what happens when we praise and worship Him?

_____

_____.

Have you looked into the face of God in worship and experienced a change of heart or a life-changing encounter with Him? _____. If you answered yes, write out a prayer describing that experience and praising God for it. If you answered no, write out a prayer asking God to show you how to worship Him in spirit and in truth. Tell Him you want to experience a life-transforming encounter with Him.

8. Read Revelation 4:11 in your Bible and underline it. Above all else, why is God worthy of praise?

9. We don't worship God for what we can get, but for what we can give to Him. Even so, we always receive great blessings when we spend time praising Him. Read Acts 16:25-26 in your Bible and underline these verses. Describe what blessings and miracles happened as a result of Paul and Silas praying and praising God. _____
_____.

Do you believe when you are praising God that chains of oppression can fall off of you and any door that keeps you locked up can be opened? _____. Write out a prayer asking God to make you the kind of worshiper who experiences these kinds of miracles every time you praise Him.

10. Pray the prayer out loud on pages 107-108 in THE POWER OF A PRAYING WOMAN. Write out two or three sentences from this prayer that are the most meaningful to you at this time in your life.

$\mathcal{W}$EEK $\mathcal{E}$LEVEN

Read Chapter 11: "Lord, Bless Me in the Work I Do"
from THE POWER OF A PRAYING WOMAN

1. Read 2 Thessalonians 3:10-11 in your Bible and under-line these verses. What can happen when we don't do any work?

2. Everyone has work to do. Describe the work you do and how you feel about it. In what ways would you like to see it change or develop?

3. Is there any part of the work you do that you dread or dislike? _____. Do you look forward to the work you do with vigor, excitement, anticipation, and a sense of accomplishment and fulfillment? _____. Explain your answers.

4. Read Proverbs 14:23 in your Bible and underline it. Do you believe the work you do is profitable? _____. In what way? _____

_____.

How would you like to see it be more profitable? _____

_____.

Do you believe God wants to bless you in the work you do? _____. In light of your answers, write out a prayer asking God to bless your work in such a way as to make it more profitable. (Remember, not all profit is monetary.)

5. Write out a prayer asking God to show you if the work you are doing is His will for your life right now. Ask Him to always keep you in the center of His will with regard to the work you do and the way you do it.

6. What is your greatest dream with regard to the work you are doing now or hope to do in the future? Explain. Write out a prayer asking God to show you if this dream is His will for your life. Tell Him that if this dream is *not* His will for your life, you want Him to take it away and put a dream in your heart that is.

7. Read Psalm 90:17 in your Bible and underline it. Write out a prayer asking God to bless and establish the work of your hands and help you to be the best you can possibly be at it.

8. Read Proverbs 31:10-29 in your Bible and underline the parts that especially speak to you. List the many ways this woman worked. What were the ways she was rewarded?

9. Read Psalm 128:1-2 and Proverbs 31:30-31 in your Bible and underline them. What are the promises in these Scriptures to those who fear the Lord?

10. Pray the prayer out loud on pages 114-115 in THE POWER OF A PRAYING WOMAN. Write out two or three sentences from this prayer that are the most meaningful to you at this time in your life.

WEEK TWELVE

Read Chapter 12: "Lord, Plant Me so I Will Bear
the Fruit of Your Spirit"
from THE POWER OF A PRAYING WOMAN

1. Read Galatians 5:22-23 in your Bible and underline these
   verses. What are the fruit of the Spirit?

   1._____   2._____

   3._____   4._____

   5._____   6._____

   7._____   8._____

   9._____

2. Of all the fruit of the Spirit, which one would you like to see manifested more obviously in your life right now? _____. Write out a prayer telling God why you want that and asking Him to give you great growth in this particular area.

3. Read Galatians 5:19-21 in your Bible and underline these verses. What are the works of the flesh? What will happen if you practice such things?

4. Read Ephesians 5:11 in your Bible and underline it. According to this verse, what is the wrong thing to do?_____.
What is the right thing to do? _____.

5. Read John 15:1-8 in your Bible and underline it. Write out verses 5 and 7 in first person. (For example, "Jesus is the vine, I am the branch. If I abide in Him, and He abides in me, I will bear...")

6. In light of John 15:5-7, what is the best way to bear fruit in your life?_____
_____. What is a good way to get your prayers answered?_____
_____.

7. When you are born again and filled with the Spirit of God, the seeds of the fruit of the Spirit are planted in you. Still, you must take care to nurture and protect these seeds and give them the conditions they need in which to grow. The following three fruit of the Spirit cannot be understood in their purest form without a sovereign work of God enabling us to know His unconditional love, His joy, and His peace that passes all understanding. Next to each fruit below, write out a prayer asking God to do such a work in you that you exhibit this particular fruit of the Spirit in a noticeable way. Include in your prayers the Scripture indicated and underline it in your Bible.

Love (John 15:10)

Joy (John 15:11)

Peace (Philippians 4:7)

8. The next three fruit of the Spirit indicate the way we are supposed to act with other people. Of course we can't always act this way consistently without God's Spirit enabling us, but there *are* things we can decide to do that will help. Under each one indicated below, write a prayer asking God to grow this fruit *in* you and manifest it *through* you in a powerful way. Then ask Him to show you things you can specifically do to exhibit this fruit of the Spirit to others. Write down everything that He shows you. Remember to include the Scripture indicated and underline it in your Bible.

Patience (James 1:4)

Kindness (Colossians 3:12)

Goodness (Matthew 12:35)

9. Do you seek God for the strength to be faithful when you are tempted to be unfaithful? _____. Do you heed the quiet voice of the Holy Spirit instructing you to be gentle when you find yourself tempted to be callous, brash, or harsh? _____. Do you ask for a fresh filling of God's Spirit to give you strength to be disciplined, especially when you want what you want when you want it, no matter what the consequences to you or to others? _____. In light of your answers, write out a prayer next to each of the following fruit of the Spirit asking God to help you exhibit each of them in your life. Include the Scripture and underline it in your Bible if you haven't done so already.

Faithfulness (Luke 16:10)

Gentleness (2 Timothy 2:24)

Self-control (2 Peter 1:5-6)

10. Pray the prayer out loud on pages 122-123 in THE POWER OF A PRAYING WOMAN. Write out two or three sentences from this prayer that are the most meaningful to you at this time in your life.

WEEK THIRTEEN

Read Chapter 13: "Lord, Preserve Me
in Purity and Holiness"
from THE POWER OF A PRAYING WOMAN

1. Read James 4:4 and 1 John 2:15-16 in your Bible and underline them. What happens when you become a friend of the world? _____.
What happens when you love the things of the world? _____. Write out a prayer asking God to show you any place where you have brought things of the world into your life that have influenced you away from the things of God. Write down anything He reveals to you about that.

2. Read 1 John 3:3 and 1 Peter 1:15-16 in your Bible and underline them. According to these Scriptures, what are we supposed to do?_____

_____.

Write a prayer below asking God to show you how to purify yourself and become holy as He is holy. Ask God to clearly show you any thoughts, actions, activities, associations, or business dealings that are not righteous. Ask Him to help you identify and separate yourself from anything that is not morally or ethically pure.

3. Read Romans 8:5-7 in your Bible and underline these verses. What do people who live in the flesh do? _____

_____.

What do those who live according to the Spirit do?

_____.

What is the consequence of being fleshly or carnally minded? _____. What is the consequence of being spiritually minded? _____.

What does being carnally or fleshly minded mean to your relationship with God? (verse 8)_____

_____.

Read Galatians 6:7-8 in your Bible and underline these verses. What do you reap when you sow to the flesh? _____. What do you reap when you sow to the Spirit? _____. Write out a prayer asking God to help you examine the fruit of your life to see if there is any place where you have sowed to the flesh. (Write down anything He reveals to you.) Ask Him to help you live your life in the Spirit and not the flesh.

4. Read 1 Thessalonians 4:3-5 in your Bible and underline these verses. Our society is so permeated with sexual immorality that you can be receiving that spirit into your soul in a way that you may not even realize. It's one of the enemy's tactics to undermine the work of God in us. Society is so perverse in this area now that, by comparison, our private sexual thoughts may not seem like anything to speak of. But they keep us from the holiness God has for us. And He can't do the great things through us He desires to do if we are allowing the enemy to muddy the waters of our soul. Write out a prayer asking God to show you any place where you have allowed a spirit of immorality to enter your mind. Ask Him to keep you free from such thoughts.

5. Read Hebrews 10:10 in your Bible and underline it. When Jesus died on the cross as a sacrifice for our sins, He made those who receive Him to be sanctified (or holy). He did that once and for all, yet living in holiness is an ongoing process, a state we must choose to live in. When we give our lives to the Lord, He cleanses and purifies us and makes us ready for what He has for us to do. Write out a prayer asking God to help you understand all that Jesus accomplished for you on the cross. Ask Him to enable you to live in it.

6. Read Hebrews 12:14 in your Bible and underline it. Why is it important to pursue holiness? _____ _____. Read Psalm 24:3-4 and underline these verses in your Bible. Who may come close to God? _____ _____. Read Matthew 5:8 in your Bible and underline it. What is the reward for having a pure heart? _____. Write out a prayer asking God to help you always walk close to Him. Include Psalm 4:3 in your prayer. (For example, "Lord, I know that You have set apart for Yourself...")

7. Read 1 Thessalonians 5:23-24 in your Bible and under-line these verses. Write them out as a prayer asking God to keep you pure and holy. (For example, "Lord God of peace, sanctify me completely, and may my whole spirit, soul...")

8. Read Galatians 5:24-25 and Ephesians 1:4 in your Bible and underline them. According to these Scriptures, how are we supposed to walk?

9. Read Ephesians 4:25-32 in your Bible and underline these verses. According to them, what are the things we are supposed to do?

10. Pray the prayer out loud on pages 130-131 in THE POWER OF A PRAYING WOMAN. Write out two or three sentences from this prayer that are the most meaningful to you at this time in your life.

WEEK FOURTEEN

Read Chapter 14: "Lord, Move Me into the Purpose
for Which I Was Created"
from THE POWER OF A PRAYING WOMAN

1. Read Ephesians 1:7-12 in your Bible and underline all the things in these verses that God has given to you. List them below.

2. Read Ephesians 1:15-21 in your Bible and underline all the things God has for you. Describe in your own words what Paul is praying will happen for you.

3. Do you believe your life has purpose? _____. Do you have a sense of what that purpose is? _____. If you answered yes to those questions, write out a prayer telling God what you believe your purpose is, and then ask Him to confirm that to you by giving you an even clearer understanding of how He wants to develop His purposes in your life. If you answered no to either question, write out a prayer asking God to show you what your purpose is. Write down anything He reveals to you or what you see as a possible direction for your life.

4. Read Romans 11:29 and 12:6-8 in your Bible and underline them. List below every talent, gift, or ability you
   have. Be generous and honest with yourself and don't
   overlook any possibility. (For example, teaching, playing
   the piano, displaying leadership skills, organizing, man-
   aging, selling, making cookies, cleaning house, or
   showing kindness, compassion, or encouragement.) It
   doesn't matter if your talent is developed or whether you
   have even used it much. Ask God to show you every gift
   He has put within you that can bless others. It won't
   make you prideful to see the gifts God has put within you;
   it will make you joyful and grateful to the Lord.

5. Read Psalm 20:4 in your Bible and underline it. Write
   out a prayer thanking God for the gifts He has placed
   within you. Tell Him you want to use those gifts for His
   glory. Name specific ones from the section above that
   are especially important to you. Ask Him to show you
   how to develop them further.

6. Read Matthew 16:25 in your Bible and underline it. What is the deepest dream of your heart? Describe it and then write out a prayer surrendering that dream to the Lord. Ask Him to either take the dream out of your heart if it is not part of His will for your life or make the dream become a reality in His way and His time. Remember, God doesn't want us to cling to our dreams. He wants us to surrender our dreams and cling to *Him*. When we cling to *Him*, He can lift us above our circumstances and our abilities and help us to accomplish far more than we ever could on our own.

7. Predestination means your _____ has
   already been _____. The Bible says we are
   predestined according to God's _____ and
   _____. That means God knows where you
   are _____ to be _____. And He knows
   how to _____ _____ _____.
   But even though you have a _____ and a
   _____, you can't get to it without being
   _____ to the _____ who _____
   it to _____ in the first place.
   When you don't _____ _____ to the one
   who _____ your _____, then in one
   moment of _____, such as _____ or
   _____, you can _____ ____ _____.
   (See page 135, first paragraph under "Know Who You
   Are and Where You Are Going" in THE POWER OF A
   PRAYING WOMAN.) According to Jeremiah 9:23-24, what
   are we to glory in? _____

   _____

   What are we *not* to glory in? _____

   _____

   (See page 136 in THE POWER OF A PRAYING WOMAN.)

8. Read 2 Peter 1:10 in your Bible and underline it. God has
   called you to do something with your life to serve Him
   and others. In the body of Christ, "every part does its
   share" and this "causes growth of the body for the edi-
   fying of itself in love" (Ephesians 4:16). Do you know
   what your calling is? _____. If you answered yes, describe
   your calling, or ministry to others, as you understand it
   right now. Write out a prayer asking God to confirm that
   to you and guide you as you fulfill it. If you answered no
   and don't believe you have a calling or ministry yet, describe how you would like to be used of the Lord. Then
   write out a prayer asking God to reveal to you if that's

what He wants you to do in the way of service to Him. Ask Him to show you clearly what your calling is. Write down whatever He shows you.

9. Read Psalm 20:4 again in your Bible. Do you have a sense of peace and trust in God's timing with regard to your purpose and call, or do you feel frustrated because you aren't where you think you should be? Write out a prayer telling God how you feel regarding that issue, and thank Him that He will fulfill His purpose in your life. Use Psalm 20:4 in your prayer.

10. Pray the prayer out loud on pages 138-140 in THE POWER OF A PRAYING WOMAN. Write out two or three sentences from this prayer that are the most meaningful to you at this time in your life.

WEEK FIFTEEN

Read Chapter 15: "Lord, Guide Me in All My
Relationships" from THE POWER OF A PRAYING WOMAN

1. Below are "Seven Good Signs of a Desirable Friend."
   Next to each sign, indicate whether you believe you have
   that kind of friend in your life and describe that person.
   If you do not have a person in your life who exhibits that
   quality, write out a prayer asking God to bring a friend
   like that into your life or bring out that quality in one of
   the friends you already have. Ask Him to help you be
   that kind of friend to others. (See pages 144-145 in THE
   POWER OF A PRAYING WOMAN.)

   A desirable friend is a person who:

   1. Tells you the truth in love.

   2. Gives you sound advice.

3. Refines you.

4. Helps you grow in wisdom.

5. Stays close to you.

6. Loves you and stands by you.

7. Is a help in time of trouble.

2. Do you believe that you exhibit to others the seven signs of a desirable friend? In which one of those qualities do you feel strongest?_____.
In which one of those qualities do you feel weakest?
_____. Write out a prayer asking God to help you in the areas where you are weakest so that you can become the kind of friend God wants you to be.

3. Read Proverbs 12:26 in your Bible and underline it. Use this verse in a prayer asking God to guide you in all your relationships so that you will have godly, uplifting, encouraging, and faithful friends. Ask Him to help you be that kind of friend to others.

4. Do you have friends who exhibit any of the negative characteristics listed in the "Seven Signs of an *Undesirable* Friend" on pages 145-146 in THE POWER OF A PRAYING WOMAN? _____. If you answered yes, pray for those friends to either turn to God and be transformed or, if necessary, taken out of your life. If you answered no, pray that neither you nor any of your friends will ever become that kind of person.

5. Read Ephesians 4:31-32 again in your Bible. Do you have a distant, troubled, or indifferent relationship with someone in your family? Describe the relationship the way it is now and what changes would you like to see happen. Write out a prayer asking God to bless your relationship with that person and remove any obstacle that keeps it from being all it should be. Ask God to work forgiveness in each of your hearts and establish good communication.

6. List the most important relationships in your life. Write out a prayer asking God to bless each of those relationships. Pray that they will grow and be preserved and that nothing will destroy them.

7. Read Ecclesiastes 4:9-12 in your Bible and underline these verses. Why is it good to be in fellowship with other believers?

8. Read Psalm 68:6 in your Bible and underline it. Are you a member of a church where you are part of a spiritual family with whom you feel connected? _____. If you answered yes, describe what is most important to you about your spiritual family. Write out a prayer asking God to bless your church and spiritual family and the relationships you have there. If you answered no to the question, write out a prayer asking God to help you find the church and spiritual family where you belong.

9. Why is it important to be yoked with people who walk closely with God? (See page 143, first paragraph, in THE POWER OF A PRAYING WOMAN.)

Why does your enemy not want you to be in a spiritual family, and why should you cover your spiritual family relationships in prayer? (See page 143, last paragraph.)

Why is it important to not be isolated? (See page 147, last paragraph.)

10. Pray the prayer out loud on pages 147-149 in THE POWER OF A PRAYING WOMAN. Write out two or three sentences from this prayer that are the most meaningful to you at this time in your life.

WEEK SIXTEEN

Read Chapter 16: "Lord, Keep Me in the Center
of Your Will" from THE POWER OF A PRAYING WOMAN

1. Read the following verses and underline them in your
   Bible. Next to each one listed below, write what the reward is for following the will of God.

   1 John 2:17

   Matthew 7:21

   Hebrews 10:36

2. Read Isaiah 30:21 in your Bible and underline it. Write out a prayer asking God to help you always hear His voice leading you so that you will not get off the path. Include this verse in your prayer.

3. Does having trouble in your life always mean you are out of God's will? Explain. How does God use the trouble in your life? (See page 152, second paragraph, in THE POWER OF A PRAYING WOMAN.)

4. Does following God's will mean that life will always be easy? _____. Whose life confirms that? _____.
How did His life confirm that? _____

_____.

Why did Jesus come down from heaven? _____

_____

(See page 152, third paragraph, in THE POWER OF A PRAYING WOMAN.)

5. Does following the will of God mean you will never feel stretched or uncomfortable? _____. (See page 153, first paragraph, in THE POWER OF A PRAYING WOMAN.) When was the last time you felt stretched and uncomfortable? Describe it. Have you ever felt stretched or uncomfortable even when you were doing what God called you to do? Explain.

6. Can you expect to sit back and do nothing and still end up in the will of God? Why or why not? (See page 153, second paragraph, in THE POWER OF A PRAYING WOMAN.)

7. Do you feel you are in the center of God's will in every area of your life right now? Explain why or why not. List any area of your life where you have uncertainty about that and write out a prayer asking God to help you know His will regarding this area of your life.

8. Write a prayer next to each of the following categories and ask God to show you if you are in the center of His will regarding these areas of your life.

Where you live.

Where you work.

What you do with your free time.

Where you go to church.

Who your relationships are with.

How you conduct each of your relationships.

What you look at or listen to.

How you serve the Lord.

How you handle your finances.

How you make decisions.

9. Do you believe that the way you determine your goals and the direction for your life is in line with God's will for you?_____. Explain your answer. Then write out a prayer asking God to align your goals and direction with His will.

10. Pray the prayer out loud on page 154 in THE POWER OF A PRAYING WOMAN. Write out two or three sentences from this prayer that are the most meaningful to you at this time in your life.

WEEK SEVENTEEN

Read Chapter 17: "Lord, Protect Me and All I Care About"
from THE POWER OF A PRAYING WOMAN

1. Can you think of an occasion when you know God protected you? Describe that time and write a prayer thanking God for His protection over you. If you can't think of such a time, ask God to show you what you are not seeing. The fact that you are still alive means God has protected you.

2. Write out a prayer thanking God for all the times He has protected you that you are not even aware of, and ask Him to continue to protect you in the future.

3. Read Psalm 91:1-4 in your Bible and underline the promises of God to you. List those promises below.

4. Read Psalm 91:5-8 in your Bible and underline the promises of God to you. List them below.

5. Read Psalm 91:9-12 in your Bible and underline the promises of God to you. List them below.

6. Read Psalm 91:13-16 in your Bible and underline the promises of God to you. List them below.

7. Read Isaiah 54:17 in your Bible and underline the promises of God there for you. Put a star next to the verse. Write the first sentence of this verse out in first person as many times as you can fit in the space provided below. (For example, "No weapon formed against me will prosper.") Speak aloud what you have written and proclaim God's promise to you.

8. Read Psalm 31:19-20 in your Bible and underline these verses. What has God promised to do for those who trust and fear Him? _____ _____. Write this Scripture out in your own words.

9. Read Psalm 119:117 in your Bible and underline it. What do you feel is your main area of vulnerability? What is your greatest concern with regard to being kept safe? What do you most need to be protected from? Describe your answers in a prayer to God and ask Him to keep you safe and protected.

10. Pray the prayer out loud on pages 160-161 in THE POWER OF A PRAYING WOMAN. Write out two or three sentences from this prayer that are the most meaningful to you at this time in your life.

$\mathcal{W}$EEK $\mathcal{E}$IGHTEEN

Read Chapter 18: "Lord, Give Me Wisdom to Make Right Decisions" from THE POWER OF A PRAYING WOMAN

1. Read Proverbs 2:3-6 in your Bible and underline these verses. According to this section of Scripture, how can you get wisdom, understanding, and discernment?

2. List the ten ways to walk in wisdom found on pages 165-166 in THE POWER OF A PRAYING WOMAN. Then write out the Scriptures indicated below.

    1. _____

    _____

    _____

    _____.

    (Proverbs 2:1-2,5)

2. _____

_____

_____

_____.

(James 1:5)

3. _____

_____

_____

_____.

(Proverbs 3:6)

4. _____

_____

_____

_____.

(Proverbs 9:10)

5. _____

_____

_____

_____.

(Proverbs 22:17)

6. _____
_____
_____
_____.

(Proverbs 4:5-6)

7. _____
_____
_____
_____.

(Proverbs 2:7)

8. _____
_____
_____
_____.

(Proverbs 11:2)

9. _____
_____
_____
_____.

(Proverbs 11:12)

10. _____
_____
_____
_____.

(1 Corinthians 1:20-21)

3. In which of these ways to walk in wisdom above do you need to most improve? Write out a prayer asking God to help you to grow and be strong in those ways.

4. Wisdom means having clear _____ and _____. It means knowing how to apply the _____ in every _____. It is discerning what is _____ and _____. It's having good _____. It's being able to _____ when you are getting too _____ to the _____. It's making the right _____ or _____. And only _____ _____what that is. "When He, the _____ of _____ has come, He will _____ you into _____ _____; for He will not _____ on His _____ _____, but whatever He _____ He will _____; and He will _____ you _____to _____." (See page 165, first paragraph, in THE POWER OF A PRAYING WOMAN.)

5. Read Psalm 1:1 again in your Bible. What must you do to be blessed?

6. According to Psalm 1:2-3, what is the reward for de-
lighting in God's laws and relying on godly counsel?

7. Of the "Ten Good Reasons to Ask for Wisdom" on pages
166-167 in THE POWER OF A PRAYING WOMAN, list the
five that are most important to you. Then write out the
Scriptures below them.

1. _____

_____

_____

_____.

2. _____

_____

_____

_____.

3. _____

_____

_____

_____.

4. _____

_____

_____

_____.

5. _____

_____

_____

_____.

8. Write out a prayer asking God to show you any way in which you are standing in the path of sinners, walking in the counsel of ungodly people, or being influenced by people who do not have godly wisdom. Write down whatever He reveals to you about that.

9. Read Ephesians 1:15-19 again in your Bible. What did Paul pray for the Ephesians?_____
_____.

Why did he want them to have wisdom? _____
_____.

Write out a prayer asking God for the same things Paul asked for the Ephesians.

10. Pray the prayer out loud on pages 168-169 in THE POWER OF A PRAYING WOMAN. Write out two or three sentences from this prayer that are the most meaningful to you at this time in your life.

$\mathcal{W}$EEK $\mathcal{N}$INETEEN

Read Chapter 19: "Lord, Deliver Me from Every Evil Work"
from THE POWER OF A PRAYING WOMAN

1. Is there anything in your life or in yourself you would like
   God to deliver you from? Explain. Write out a prayer
   asking God to set you free from those things.

2. Look up the following Scriptures that explain how deliverance can be found and write them in the space below.

   By praying for it (Psalm 71:12).

   By crying out to God for it (Psalm 34:17).

By knowing God's truth (John 8:32).

By spending time in the Lord's presence
(2 Corinthians 3:17).

By fearing God (Psalm 34:7).

3. Read Galatians 5:1 in your Bible and underline it. Write it out below as a prayer to God, asking Him to help you remember to do what it says every time you get discouraged. (For example, "Lord, help me to stand fast in the liberty...")

4. Do you now or have you ever felt as though you were sliding back into the very thing from which you have already been set free? Explain. Be specific. Were you really going backwards or was God taking you to a new level of deliverance and freedom? If you don't know, write out a prayer asking God to show you.

5. Read 2 Corinthians 1:9-10 in your Bible and underline these verses. What are the great truths here about God delivering you or setting you free?

6. Read Philippians 1:6 in your Bible and underline it. What is the promise to you in this verse?_____
   _____
   _____.

   Write out a prayer thanking God for this promise. Be specific.

7. Read Psalm 34:19 and Proverbs 21:31 in your Bible and underline them. According to these Scriptures, who is your Deliverer? _____. Write out a prayer thanking God that He is your Deliverer. Include these Scriptures in your prayer.

8. Answer the following questions about your life. If your answer to any of the questions is no, explain your reason why. If you answered yes, write out a prayer telling God how you feel and ask Him to deliver you in this area.

Do you ever feel distant from God? _____.

Do you ever feel as though your prayers are not being heard or answered? _____.

Do you feel discouraged and sad more than you feel joyful and happy? _____.

Do you have habits you can't seem to break? _____.

Do you have reoccurring negative thoughts? _____.

Do you feel bad about yourself? _____.

Do you have continual strife or difficulty in your relationships? _____.

Do you have constant financial problems year after year? _____.

Are you often drawn toward things that are not good for you? _____.

Do you have trouble getting your eyes off of your problems and onto God? _____.

9. Read 2 Timothy 4:18 in your Bible and underline it. Write out a prayer asking God to deliver you from every evil work and show you any time you need to be set free from something.

10. Pray the prayer out loud on pages 175-176 in THE POWER OF A PRAYING WOMAN. Write out two or three sentences from this prayer that are the most meaningful to you at this time in your life.

$\mathcal{W}$EEK $\mathcal{T}$WENTY

Read Chapter 20: "Lord, Set Me Free from Negative Emotions" from THE POWER OF A PRAYING WOMAN

1. Are you suffering with any degree of anxiety over anything? Explain. If you are not anxious about anything now, what have you been anxious about in the past, and how did you get rid of your anxiety? Describe the feelings you have physically and emotionally when you are anxious.

2. Read Philippians 4:6-7 in your Bible and underline these verses. Write this Scripture out below as a prayer that you could pray whenever you feel anxious. (For example, "Lord, I pray that You would help me to be anxious for nothing...")

3. Read Psalm 94:19 and Luke 12:29-31 in your Bible and underline them. Next to them in the margin of your Bible, write the word "anxiety" and draw a star. Under each verse below, write in your own words what it means to you with regard to any anxiety you may experience now or in the future.

Psalm 94:19

Luke 12:29-31

4. Read Ephesians 4:26-27 and Ecclesiastes 7:9 in your Bible and underline them. Write out a prayer below confessing any anger you may have now or have struggled with in the past. Ask God to set you free from it so that you won't miss what He has for you. If you are not aware of any anger in you, ask God to reveal any place in your heart where you have hidden anger so you can be delivered from it. Include these two sections of Scripture in your prayer.

5. Read Philippians 4:11-13 in your Bible and underline these verses. Write out a prayer confessing any times you have been dissatisfied in your life. Be specific. Ask God to help you trust His ability to take care of you and get you where you need to go. Ask Him to help you find rest and peace in the midst of any situation. Include verses 11 and 13 in your prayer.

6. Read James 3:16, 1 Corinthians 3:3, and Proverbs 14:30 in your Bible and underline them. According to these Scriptures, what is the result of envy? _____

_____

_____.

We are all susceptible to envy at some time. Constantly comparing yourself to others and feeling as though you come up short is a form of envy. What is it that tempts you to be envious? Write out a prayer asking God to keep you free of envy. Confess anything you see in yourself that could be the beginning of envy. Better to get it out on paper than to let it grow into something that keeps you from all God has for you. I know it is embarrassing to admit these things but remember, God already knows. He is just waiting to hear it from you so you can be free.

7. Read Psalm 107:13-14 in your Bible and underline these
   verses. What do they say to do when you are troubled?
   _____.

   What does God do in return? _____
   _____
   _____.

   Do you ever suffer with depression? If so, is there anything
   in particular that triggers it? Explain. (I'm not talking
   about a physical imbalance here. If you feel you have that,
   see a doctor.) Write out a prayer asking God to lift you out
   of depression. Tell the enemy of your soul that he has no
   power to bring a blanket of depression over you because
   God is your Deliverer and has delivered you of that.

8. Read Acts 8:23 and Hebrews 12:15 in your Bible and underline them. According to these Scriptures, what does bitterness do to us? _____

_____

_____.

Bitterness is characterized by intense and distressful hostility. It is painful and fierce. And it can simmer underneath the surface of our carefully manicured exterior, eating away our insides like a cancerous growth. Are you aware of any bitterness in you? Write out a prayer below asking God to expose any root of bitterness in you and destroy it. Ask Him to always keep you far from bitterness in your life.

9. Hopelessness is a _____ _____ that will eventually affect the _____ of your _____ and _____. But when you deliberately _____ to put your _____ in the _____, He will meet all your_____and take all _____ away. Just as we can _____ what _____ we will have every day, we can _____ to put our _____ in _____. We can _____ our _____. (See page 183, last paragraph, in THE POWER OF A PRAYING WOMAN.)

Write out the following Scriptures about hope:

Colossians 1:27

Romans 5:5

Psalm 130:7

Psalm 119:147

Psalm 71:5

Psalm 39:7

Hopelessness is a snare to your soul. Write out a prayer asking God to help you always find your hope in Him.

10. Pray the prayer out loud on pages 184-185 in THE POWER OF A PRAYING WOMAN. Write out two or three sentences from this prayer that are the most meaningful to you at this time in your life.

WEEK TWENTY-ONE

Read Chapter 21: "Lord, Comfort Me in Times of Trouble" from THE POWER OF A PRAYING WOMAN

1. Read 1 Peter 4:12-13 in your Bible and underline these verses. Write this section of Scripture out in your own words and explain what it means to your life.

2. Read 1 Peter 5:10 and Matthew 5:3-4 in your Bible and underline them. What does God promise to do as a result of your suffering?

3. What is the most difficult time you have experienced in your life since you became a believer? Describe that time. Was your faith in God strengthened through it? Why or why not?

4. Have you ever gone through a difficult time yet you saw the power of God revealed *in* it and the Lord glorified *through* it? Explain. If you can't think of such an example, write out a prayer asking God to do just that whenever you are in a time of suffering or grief.

5. Read 1 Peter 4:1 in your Bible and underline it. Have you ever gone through a difficult time, but when it was over you knew God had purified you and you were walking closer with Him as a result? Explain. If you can't think of an example from your life, write a prayer asking God to do this whenever you are in a time of grief or suffering.

6. Read Hebrews 12:11 in your Bible and underline it. Have you ever gone through a difficult time and now, looking back, you believe God was disciplining, pruning, chastening, or teaching you something in the process? Explain. If you can't think of an example from your life, write a prayer asking God to reveal to you what He is doing in your life whenever you are going through a difficult time.

7. Have you ever gone through a time of struggle, suffering, or grief but you knew it was the enemy's attack upon you? Explain. Regardless of your answer, write out a prayer asking God to help you clearly recognize whenever you are being attacked by the enemy. Ask Him to teach you how to stand strong in the midst of it.

8. Read 2 Corinthians 4:8-11 and 17-18 in your Bible and underline these verses. Describe in your own words what these Scriptures mean for you and your life, and what you can be thankful for in the midst of any trials you go through.

9. Look up the following Scriptures in your Bible and underline them if you haven't already done so. Write them out below and underline the promise to you in each one.

   Matthew 5:3

   Matthew 5:4

   Matthew 5:5

   Matthew 5:6

   Matthew 5:7

   Matthew 5:10

10. Pray the prayer out loud on pages 190-191 in THE POWER OF A PRAYING WOMAN. Write out two or three sentences from this prayer that are the most meaningful to you at this time in your life.

$\mathcal{W}$EEK $\mathcal{T}$WENTY-$\mathcal{T}$WO

Read Chapter 22: "Lord, Enable Me to Resist the Temptation to Sin" from THE POWER OF A PRAYING WOMAN

1. What is your greatest area of temptation? How difficult is the struggle you have, and how have you been able to handle it?

2. Read 1 Corinthians 10:13 in your Bible and underline it. Is the temptation you face any different than what other people have faced? Why?

3. Write out a prayer telling God of your greatest area of temptation or struggle and ask Him to set you free from the grip of it. Be specific.

4. Read 1 Corinthians 10:12 in your Bible and underline it. List as many times as you can think of when you have been tempted to do what God has said not to do. Write out a prayer asking God to free and protect you from these temptations.

5. Read Galatians 5:1 again in your Bible. What can you do when you are faced with temptation? What could you do that would help you stand strong? (For example, be in the Word every day, and so on.)

6. Read Matthew 26:41 in your Bible and underline it. What does Jesus want you to do so that you won't enter into temptation? _____.
Which part of us is strong? _____. Which part of us is weak? _____. Write out a prayer asking God to help you pray and be watchful over areas where you can be tempted.

7. Have you felt, or are you feeling now, any sexual temptation? If so, speak a prayer of confession and repentance to
God for any improper sexual thoughts or actions and ask
Him to set you completely free from it. Whether you are
tempted that way or not, write out a prayer asking God to
keep your mind and body free from any sexual sin. Ask
Him to take all temptation away from you before it even
presents itself. Ask God to protect you from a spirit of
lust.

8. Read James 1:12 in your Bible and underline it. What is
your reward for enduring temptation and not falling into
it?

9. Answer the following questions about temptation. (See pages 195-197 in THE POWER OF A PRAYING WOMAN.)

Who can be tempted?

What things can you be tempted by?

When can you be tempted?

Where can you be tempted?

Why might you be tempted?

How might you be tempted?

When is the best time to pray about temptation? (Page 197)

What did Jesus teach us to pray regarding temptation?
(Matthew 6:13)

Can you ever be immune to temptation? (Page 197)

What did Jesus instruct His disciples to do?
(Luke 22:46)

When did Jesus' temptation happen? (See page 197,
last paragraph.)

Why do you have the power to overcome temptation?
(1 John 4:4)

10. Pray the prayer out loud on page 198 in THE POWER OF A
PRAYING WOMAN. Write out two or three sentences from
this prayer that are the most meaningful to you at this
time in your life.

$\mathcal{W}$EEK $\mathcal{T}$WENTY-$\mathcal{T}$HREE

Read Chapter 23: "Lord, Heal Me and Help Me Care for My Body" from THE POWER OF A PRAYING WOMAN

1. Read 1 Corinthians 6:19-20 in your Bible and underline these verses. What is the main reason to take care of your body?

2. What are your greatest areas of struggle with regard to taking care of your body? Explain and be specific.

3. Write out a prayer asking God to help you be disciplined in the areas of body care you mentioned above. Be specific.

4. Is there any area of your body that needs healing today? If so, write out a prayer asking God to heal you. Include Jeremiah 17:14 in your prayer and thank God that He is your Healer. If you do not need healing, write a prayer thanking God for that and asking Him to protect you from sickness, disease, accidents, and infirmity.

5. Read Mark 6:56 in your Bible and underline it. According to this verse, who was healed? _____ _____. In what ways could you touch Jesus today and find healing for your body?

6. Read James 5:14-16 in your Bible and underline these verses. What are those who need healing supposed to do?

7. Read Psalm 103:1-3 again in your Bible. Write this section of Scripture out as a prayer of thanksgiving to the Lord. (For example, "Lord, I bless You with all my soul. Everything that is in me blesses...")

8. Read Exodus 15:26 in your Bible and underline it. If God is the same yesterday, today, and forever as He says He is (Hebrews 13:8), what is the promise to you in this Scripture, and what are God's requirements?

9. Read Acts 14:8-10 and Matthew 9:20-22 in your Bible
   and underline them. What do these two sections of
   Scripture have in common?_____
   _____.

   What was required of these people for them to be
   healed?_____.
   Write out a prayer asking God to help you always have
   faith to believe for your own healing and for the healing
   of others for whom you pray.

10. Pray the prayer out loud on pages 205-206 in THE POWER
    OF A PRAYING WOMAN. Write out two or three sentences
    from this prayer that are the most meaningful to you at
    this time in your life.

$\mathcal{W}$EEK $\mathcal{T}$WENTY-$\mathcal{F}$OUR

Read Chapter 24: "Lord, Free Me from Ungodly Fear"
from THE POWER OF A PRAYING WOMAN

1. Read 1 John 4:18 in your Bible and underline it. What is
true of someone who has fear?_____
_____.
What casts out all fear? _____.
Complete the following sentence in detail. "Lord, some-
times I have fear about…" Then write out a prayer asking
God to take that fear and replace it with His love.

2. Read 2 Timothy 1:7 in your Bible and underline it. Write out a prayer below thanking God that He has not given you a spirit of fear. Thank Him for what He *has* given you as promised in this Scripture.

3. Read Psalm 27:1 and 3 in your Bible and underline these verses. Write them out below as your own declaration of faith.

4. Is there anything in particular that triggers fear in you? _____. If you answered yes, tell God the things that bring fear to your heart. Don't worry about how bizarre or remote the possibility of these things may sound. Name them before the Lord so that they will lose their power. Ask Him to set you free from them. If you answered no, write out a prayer asking God to keep you free from fear.

5. Have you ever had a fear or dread of something that actually came true, but the fear of it turned out to be worse than the actual experience? Explain your answer. Has God ever used your fear for good, such as calling you to pray or to take necessary action? Explain.

6. What would you do differently with your life if you could live without any fear? Explain.

7. What are the two kinds of fear? _____ and _____. List the four ways to get rid of ungodly fear. (See pages 210-211 in THE POWER OF A PRAYING WOMAN.)

1. _____.

2. _____

   _____.

3. _____.

4. _____

   _____.

Are you doing all four of these things? _____ Which ones do you feel you need to do better? _____
_____.
Write out a prayer asking God to help you improve in these areas.

8. What are seven good things that come from fearing God? (See pages 212-213 in THE POWER OF A PRAYING WOMAN.)

1. _____.

2. _____.

3. _____.

4. _____.

5. _____.

6. _____.

7. _____.

Which of the blessings listed above are you most in need of right now? _____
_____.

Write out the Scriptures that pertains to those particular blessings.

9. Read Proverbs 1:28-30 in your Bible and underline these
   verses. What is the reason God will not answer our
   prayers? _____

   _____

   _____.

   Read Proverbs 2:3-5 again in your Bible. How can you
   understand the fear of the Lord and find the knowledge
   of God? _____

   _____

   _____.

10. Pray the prayer out loud on pages 213-214 in THE POWER
    OF A PRAYING WOMAN. Write out two or three sentences
    from this prayer that are the most meaningful to you at
    this time in your life.

Week Twenty-Five

Read Chapter 25: "Lord, Use Me to Touch the Lives of Others" from THE POWER OF A PRAYING WOMAN

1. Read 1 Peter 4:10 in your Bible and underline it. List all the gifts, talents, and abilities you have that could be used to help others. Be generous with yourself. If you are not sure about your gifts and talents or you are having a hard time thinking of them, ask God to show you. You may have abilities that *you* don't think are valuable, but would be a great blessing to *others*.

2. Write out a prayer asking God to reveal to you any talents and abilities you have that you are *not* aware of that could be used to bless others. Write down whatever He shows you and anything you can think of. (For example, cooking, driving, planting, painting, sharing, helping, communicating, cleaning, serving, and so on.)

3. Out of the two lists above, choose what you believe to be your three strongest gifts, talents, or abilities, and write a prayer below asking God to enable you to use them for His glory in ways beyond what you have ever dreamed. Be bold in your asking.

4. Out of the two lists on the previous page, choose three talents or abilities that you have hardly used but would like to use in a more powerful way. Write out a prayer below naming them before the Lord and asking Him to show you how to use those abilities for His glory.

5. Read 1 John 3:17-19 in your Bible and underline these verses. Write out a prayer asking God to show you someone who has a need you could meet in some way. (For example, telling someone about Jesus, giving them money, making a phone call to or for them, giving them a book, taking them some place they need to go, making them food, praying for them, asking what you can do to help them, and so on.) Did God show you some things to do? If so, write them down.

172 of a Praying Woman Study Guide

Do one or more of the things God showed you in the question on the previous page, or that came to your mind to do. Describe what you did. What was the result? How did the other person react? How did you feel afterward?

6. There is never a time when we don't need encouragement from the Lord. God gives us encouragement whenever we need it in His Word. We also find it in His presence, where there is fullness of joy (Psalm 16:11). It can happen when your spirit touches God's Spirit in praise and worship. Write out the ways in which God has encouraged you lately. Then write out a prayer thanking Him for that. Tell Him in what ways you *need* encouragement. Ask Him to show you how you can be an encouragement to others around you.

7. Read Galatians 6:9 in your Bible and underline it. What does God say about doing good? _____

_____

_____.

   Read Hebrews 6:10-12 in your Bible and underline these verses. Write this Scripture out in your own words. What does it say to you specifically?

8. Prayer is the_____ _____we can give to _____. We can never move into all _____ _____ _____ _____ until we first move into _____ prayer. (See page 219, second and third paragraphs, in THE POWER OF A PRAYING WOMAN.) Write out a prayer asking God to teach you how to pray for others and help you move deeper into intercessory prayer than you have ever been before.

9. Read 1 Corinthians 10:24 in your Bible and underline it. Write out a prayer asking God to show you whom He wants you to pray for at this time. Below that, write down everyone's name He brings to your mind. Over the next week, lift those people up in prayer. Ask God to show you specifically how to pray for each one and write down what He shows you next to their name.

10. Pray the prayer out loud on pages 220-221 in THE POWER OF A PRAYING WOMAN. Write out two or three sentences from this prayer that are the most meaningful to you at this time in your life.

Week Twenty-Six

Read Chapter 26: "Lord, Train Me to Speak Only Words That Bring Life" from THE POWER OF A PRAYING WOMAN

1. Read Matthew 12:34 in your Bible and underline it. How could you fill your heart so that it overflows with good and positive things? In what way would that affect the words that come out of your mouth? Explain.

2. Read Philippians 2:14-15 in your Bible and underline these verses. Do you complain very much? Explain. Whether you are a complainer or not, write this portion of Scripture out as a prayer to God. (For example, "Lord, help me to do all things without...")

3. Read Philippians 4:8 in your Bible and underline it. Next to the following list of things we are supposed to think about, write the words that mean the same thing. (See pages 225 and 226 in THE POWER OF A PRAYING WOMAN.)

- Whatever things are true: (honest, genuine, and so on)

  _____

  _____.

- Whatever things are noble:

  _____

  _____.

- Whatever things are just:

  _____

  _____.

- Whatever things are pure:

  _____

  _____.

- Whatever things are lovely:

  _____

  _____.

- Whatever things are of good report:

  _____

  _____.

- Whatever things are virtuous:

  _____

  _____.

- Whatever things are praiseworthy:

  _____

  _____.

4. What are the five things that happen when a wise woman speaks? (See pages 226-228 in THE POWER OF A PRAYING WOMAN.) List below.

When a wise woman speaks:

1. _____.

2. _____.

3. _____.

4. _____.

5. _____.

In which of these five ways a wise woman speaks do you feel you most need to improve? Write out a prayer asking God to help you in all of those areas, but especially the area where you feel weakest.

5. Read 1 Peter 3:15 in your Bible and underline it. Write out below what you would tell someone who asked you to explain why you have hope. Be prepared to say this to someone someday.

6. Read Proverbs 29:20 in your Bible and underline it. Have there been times when you spoke too quickly and you wished you could have taken your words back? Describe one of those times and write out a prayer asking God to forgive you and help you to be sensitive to the Holy Spirit when you speak.

7. Read Ephesians 4:25 again in your Bible. Write out a prayer asking God to make you a strong woman of truth so that you always speak the truth in every situation. Ask Him to give you the sensitivity and discernment to know when it is better to not say anything at all.

8. Read Matthew 12:36-37 in your Bible and underline these verses. What do they say about the words we speak?

_____

_____

_____.

Write out a prayer asking God to show you if and when you talk too much. Write down what He shows you about yourself. Pray that He will enable you to always speak words that have meaning and purpose. If you can think of times when you spoke words you wish you hadn't, mention those to God and ask Him to redeem those times in some way.

9. Read Ecclesiastes 10:12-13 in your Bible and underline these verses. What kind of person speaks graciously?

_____.

What is the result of speaking foolishly and not graciously?

_____

_____. Write out a prayer asking God to enable you to speak graciously to *all* people at *all* times.

10. Pray the prayer out loud on pages 228-229 in THE POWER OF A PRAYING WOMAN. Write out two or three sentences from this prayer that are the most meaningful to you at this time in your life.

WEEK TWENTY-SEVEN

Read Chapter 27: "Lord, Transform Me into a Woman of
Mountain-Moving Faith"
from THE POWER OF A PRAYING WOMAN

1. God takes the _____ bit of _____ we have
and makes it _____ into something _____
when we _____ _____ _____. The Bible says
that "God has _____" to each one a _____
of _____" (Romans 12:3). We already have
_____ _____ to start with. When we
_____ _____ in that _____, God
_____ our _____. In other words, acting
in _____ begets _____ _____.
(See page 231, last paragraph in THE POWER OF A
PRAYING WOMAN.)

2. Read Hebrews 11:6 in your Bible and underline it. According to this verse, how is it possible to please God?

3. Read 1 Peter 1:6-7 in your Bible and underline these verses. According to these verses, what is one of the reasons we go through trials?

4. Read Matthew 6:25-30 in your Bible and underline verses 25, 27, and 30. Have you experienced times when you felt your faith was weak yet God answered your prayers and provided for you in your need anyway? Did this increase your faith in God's grace, goodness, and love for you? Explain. If you do not recall any such time, write out a prayer asking God to strengthen your faith and enable you to experience His mercy, blessings, and answers to your prayers.

5. Read Romans 10:17 again in your Bible. According to this verse, what is one of the best ways to grow in faith? Can you give an example of a time when simply reading the Bible increased your faith to believe for something specific? Explain.

6. Describe the level of faith you believe you have right now.

7. Describe the level of faith you *want* to have and explain why.

8. Describe what promise of God you would like to boldly claim in faith right now. Write out a great faith-stretching prayer you would like to pray right now and see answered immediately. Ask God for the faith to believe for miracles when you pray.

9. Read Mark 9:23 in your Bible and underline it. Put two stars next to it. Write out the portion of this Scripture as it appears at the top of page 235 in THE POWER OF A PRAYING WOMAN. Write it as many times as you can in this space.

10. Pray the prayer out loud on pages 233-234 in THE POWER OF A PRAYING WOMAN. Write out two or three sentences from this prayer that are the most meaningful to you at this time in your life.

$\mathcal{W}$EEK $\mathcal{T}$WENTY-$\mathcal{E}$IGHT

Read Chapter 28: "Lord, Change Me into the Likeness of Christ" from THE POWER OF A PRAYING WOMAN

1. Read Ephesians 3:14-19 in your Bible and underline these verses. They speak of the true and ultimate restoration the Lord has for us. That kind of restoration doesn't merely enable us to obey God's laws, but it transforms us from the inside out so that our character becomes like His. Write in your own words what God has for you in this portion of Scripture. How does this affect your level of faith and hope?

2. List the seven ways we can be more like Christ. (See pages 238-241 in THE POWER OF A PRAYING WOMAN.)

We can be more like Jesus by being:

1. _____.

2. _____.

3. _____.

4. _____.

5. _____.

6. _____.

7. _____.

3. Read 1 John 3:16 in your Bible and underline it. There are very few people whom God asks to actually physically die for Him, and they are given special grace to do so. But He asks us all to die to our flesh for Him in the areas of our time, finances, activities, sacrifices, and abilities. In what ways have you died to yourself and your fleshly desires so that you could better serve Him? Explain. Write out a prayer asking God to so fill you with His love that you find it natural to lay down your life for others in whatever way He shows you.

4. Read Proverbs 16:18 in your Bible and underline it. According to this verse, what happens when we are not humble? _____.
   Write out a prayer asking God to give you a humble heart so that this won't happen to you.

5. Read Galatians 2:20 in your Bible and underline it. Write this verse out as a prayer to the Lord. (For example, "Lord, I know that I have been crucified with Christ and....") Include in your prayer the specific areas of your life where you need special help from God so your flesh will not rule you.

6. Read John 13:14-15 in your Bible and underline these verses. In what way could you serve others as Jesus did? Write out a prayer asking God to make you a giving person the way Jesus was.

7. Read 2 Corinthians 6:17-18 in your Bible and underline these verses. Describe in your own words what they ask you to do. Write out a prayer asking God to help you touch the world but not become like it, to be separate from the world yet able to do your part to change it for His glory. Ask Him to show you in what ways you can do that now. Write down what He shows you.

8. Read 2 Corinthians 12:9 and Philippians 4:13 again in your Bible. According to these Scriptures, what does God give to you in your weakness? _____.
What can *you* do in the midst of your weakness? _____
_____. Write out a prayer thanking God for the truth and promises to you in these verses.

9. Read Psalm 34:5 in your Bible and underline it. Write out a prayer asking God to crowd out any darkness in you and make your countenance appear to others as a radiant reflection of His glory. Tell Him of any times when you feel you do not radiate His beauty and light and ask Him to do a transforming work in you so that does not happen any more. (Don't worry, we all have those times.)

10. Pray the prayer out loud on pages 241-242 in THE POWER OF A PRAYING WOMAN. Write out two or three sentences from this prayer that are the most meaningful to you at this time in your life.

$\mathscr{W}$EEK $\mathscr{T}$WENTY-$\mathscr{N}$INE

Read Chapter 29: "Lord, Lift Me out of My Past"
from THE POWER OF A PRAYING WOMAN

1. The reason God doesn't want to _____ your _____
completely out of your _____ is because He
wants to _____ that part of your _____ for the
_____ He has _____ you to do. He can take
the _____ thing about your _____ and
make it to be your _____ _____ in the
_____. He will weave it into the_____
of your _____ to the _____, and out of it
you will bring the _____ of the _____ to
other people. That's why God wants you to _____
from the _____ and witness firsthand how He can
_____ _____, but He doesn't want you _____
_____. He wants you to _____ your _____
like a _____ _____, but not like a
_____ for your _____. (See page
245, first and second paragraphs, in THE POWER OF A
PRAYING WOMAN.)

195

2. Do you have any memories from your past—even as re-
cently as yesterday—that cause you pain today? Explain.

3. Can you think of anything that happened in your past
that could be keeping you from moving into all God has
for you now? Explain. Do you believe God can redeem
the past and use it for His glory?

4. Read 2 Corinthians 5:17 in your Bible and underline it. Put a star next to it and say this verse out loud five times, proclaiming it as a promise to you. Write out a prayer thanking God for this promise and include this verse in your prayer. (For example, "Lord, I thank You that because I am in Christ, I am...")

5. Read Isaiah 43:18-19 in your Bible and underline these verses. What does God say to do with the things of the past? _____ _____. What does He promise to do instead? _____ _____. What do these verses mean to you and your life right now?

6. Write out a prayer asking God to set you so free from the past that you don't even think about it except to recall your victory over it. Ask Him to use the events of your past for His glory.

7. Read Philippians 3:13-14 in your Bible and underline these verses. What are they telling you to do about your past?_____
_____.

Do you feel you are able to do that? _____. Write out a prayer asking God to help you do those things.

8. Do you suffer with any feelings of rejection or *fear* of rejection? _____. Do you avoid certain situations for fear you will be rejected? _____. Have you been rejected by anyone at any time? _____. Do you tend to interpret other people's actions or words as rejection of you? _____. If you answered yes to any of these questions, explain why and write out a prayer asking God to set you free from any form of rejection. If you answered no to all of these questions, write out a prayer thanking God for His love and your sense of His complete acceptance of you.

9. Read Ephesians 1:3-6 in your Bible and underline these verses. Write this portion of Scripture out as a prayer of thanksgiving to God for what He has done for you. Substitute "I," "me," or "my" for every pronoun, and "daughter" for the word "sons." (For example, "Thank You, Lord, that You have blessed me with every spiritual blessing...")

10. Pray the prayer out loud on page 247 in THE POWER OF A PRAYING WOMAN. Write out two or three sentences from this prayer that are the most meaningful to you at this time in your life.

$\mathcal{W}$EEK $\mathcal{T}$HIRTY

Read Chapter 30: "Lord, Lead Me into the Future You Have for Me" from THE POWER OF A PRAYING WOMAN

1. Read 1 Corinthians 2:9 in your Bible and underline it. Put a star next to it. Write this verse out below. Then write a prayer asking God to permanently implant this verse in your memory and give you faith to believe it. Thank Him that what He has for you is beyond what you can even imagine.

2. Read Jeremiah 29:11-13 in your Bible and underline these verses. Describe below the thoughts God thinks toward you. How do they make you feel about your future?

3. What are your greatest concerns with regard to your future? List them all below in a prayer to God. (For example, "Dear Lord, I am concerned about my future in the following ways...") Be specific.

4. Read Proverbs 4:18 in your Bible and underline it. Write out a prayer asking God to deliver you from all concern about your future and thanking Him for His promise that your path will only get brighter and brighter. Include this Scripture in your prayer. (For example, "Lord, I thank You that my path is like...")

5. Read Luke 18:1-8 in your Bible and underline verses 1 and 7. Write these eight verses in your own words and describe what Jesus is saying to you about your commitment to prayer.

6. Read Isaiah 55:8-12 in your Bible and underline all the verses that are especially speaking to your heart. In your own words, tell what God is speaking to you in each verse and why they make you feel more secure about your future and the life God has for you.

7. Read Deuteronomy 1:21 in your Bible and underline it. These are the words Moses spoke to Israel before they were to enter the Promised Land. What are the two things God told them *not* to do? _____ _____. *You* are going to enter the Promised Land for *your* life too, and the Lord is saying the same thing to you. He doesn't want you to be afraid or discouraged. That's because there are giants in the Promised Land that you have to battle. They are manifestations of the enemy who is trying to oppose you. God has not given you fear. It comes from the enemy. God is a God of encouragement. Only the enemy comes to discourage. Remember that the bigger the giant you face, the greater the promise God has for you and the more the enemy will try to keep you from it. The devil will try to eat away at your courage and confidence, so recognize his tactics and don't allow him the satisfaction of seeing you afraid or discouraged. Write out a prayer below asking God to bring you into the Promised Land He has for you and help you stand strong in the face of giants. List any giants—including fear and discouragement—that you feel are opposing you right now.

8. Read Luke 1:37 and Matthew 19:26 in your Bible and underline them. Put a star next to each one of them. Whenever you are threatened by the giants of doubt, fear, discouragement, and whatever else, choose to believe that anything is *possible* and nothing is *impossible* because God is with you. Write these Scriptures out below as a declaration to the enemy that you stand strong on the Word of God and nothing will keep you from the future the Lord has for you.

9. Read Psalm 23 in your Bible and underline it. In your own words, describe the promises for your future contained within this psalm.

10. Pray the prayer out loud on page 254 in THE POWER OF A PRAYING WOMAN. Write out two or three sentences from this prayer that are the most meaningful to you at this time in your life.

CANSWERS TO PRAYER

What answers to prayer have you seen since you started praying for yourself? Be sure to write them down. It's important to acknowledge what God has done and praise Him for it.

Other Books
by Stormie Omartian

The Power of a Praying® Husband
The Power of a Praying® Husband
The Power of a Praying® Husband Prayer & Study Guide
The Power of a Praying® Husband Book of Prayers

The Power of a Praying® Parent
The Power of a Praying® Parent
The Power of a Praying® Parent Prayer and Study Guide
The Power of a Praying® Parent Book of Prayers

The Power of a Praying® Wife
The Power of a Praying® Wife
The Power of a Praying® Wife Prayer and Study Guide
The Power of a Praying® Wife Audio
The Power of a Praying® Wife Book of Prayers

The Power of a Praying® Woman
The Power of a Praying® Woman
The Power of a Praying® Woman Prayer and Study Guide
The Power of a Praying® Woman Book of Prayers

The Power of Praying® Together
The Power of Praying® Together

The Prayer That Changes Everything™
The Prayer That Changes Everything™
The Prayer That Changes Everything™ Book of Prayers

Just Enough Light for the Step I'm On
Just Enough Light for the Step I'm On
Just Enough Light for the Step I'm On Book of Prayers
Just Enough Light for the Step I'm On—A Devotional
Prayer Journey

Other Items
Greater Health God's Way
Book of Prayer
Stormie
The Power of Praying®
The Power of a Praying® Teen
The Power of a Praying® Kid
The Power of a Praying® Woman Bible
Prayers for Emotional Wholeness